She lives within me

Jill Thompson

BookLeaf Publishing

Presentation by *BookLeaf Publishing*

Web: www.bookleafpub.com

E-mail: info@bookleafpub.com

ISBN: 9789357740005

First edition 2023

To My Mam on her 60th Birthday

Thank you for all you've ever done for us

Jx

I have only done all of these because of you

I sat on the bunk laughing over sugar coated
nuts,
I roll my eyes with you at Dad's ifs and but,
I ate carnation ice cream on the red hot metal
benches,
I rebuilt many, many, many fences.

I stirred the Christmas cake with nanna's spoon,
I watched many a cartoon,
I flew down a hill in a bread basket,
I had a question and knew I only had to ask it.

I cuddled cats and walked dogs,
I entered races and went for jogs,
I moved barrow upon barrow of poo,
I have only done all of these because of you

There once was a Mam from Northumberland

There once was a Mam from Northumberland
Whose daughter was not a fan of dry sand
She read Anne Frank lots
Loved squeezing big spots
And could fix, mend or botch with just one
hand.

Recipe for the bestest Mam

Ingredients

4 cups of love
3 cups of spirit
6 tablespoons of determination, whisked
2 handfuls of adventure
1.5 teaspoons of laughter
1/2 cup tickles
1 pinch of Grandma or best friend

Method

*Preheat the oven to 180°C
*In a large glass bowl, combine love, spirit and
determination. Blend at a whirlwind for 9
months, until a soft dough is formed
*In a separate, Tupperware bowl, stir adventure
until thawed. Quickly fold into main batter until
completely cuddled
*Add the laughter and knead carefully,
spreading laughter throughout the dough. *This
is the most delicate phase - too much laughter
will make the dough fall on the fall, crying
uncontrollably, but too little will result in a
lumpy dough

*Once laughter has been kneaded in, sprinkle tickles on top. This is the point in the recipe where you can add your own flair: poo picking sprinkles, corned beef pie decorations or french plaits of necessity, for example
*Bake for 38.5 years. Remove from the oven and allow to perfect
*If desired, add a pinch of Grandma or best friend for effect

My Mam and Me alphabet

A is for Alligators, we saw in Florida
B is for bread, because you love toast
C is for cillit bang, because it cleans anything
but this could have been coffee or compromise
D is for Diamonds, and Dad and dogs and
daffodils
E is for everyday, because they wouldn't be the
same without you
F is for France, because you'd never seen a
French hospital before
G is for Grace, because she goes perfectly with
Grandma and Grandad
H is for home, because home is where you are
I is for ice, or rather no ice
J is for Jill, because you made the best one
K is for kitten, because Alan obviously needs a
friend
L is for Lucy, because slobber chops loves you
M is for medal, because you deserve several
N is for Next, because we keep them in business
O is for Oz, because we've had so many
adventures
P is for poo picking, because, well – there is lots
of it!

Q is for Queen Elizabeth, because she's the only
Queen you've seen
R is for Rabbits, because there has been quite a
few
S is for Susan, and straw and shovelling and
sugared almonds
T is for toilets, the kind that fall off hotel walls
U is for Umbrellas, because you can never have
enough
V is for Vegas, because we'll never forget that
helicopter flight
W is for wedding day, a day you helped make
magical
X is for x-ray, please see the letter F
Y is for yarn, because you can teach crochet at
10pm
Z is for zig-zag scissors, because you are the
queen of crafting

The fluffy, warm dressing gown

Whose dressing gown is that? I think I know.
Its owner is quite quiet though.
Out for the day waiting for a vivid rainbow,
I watch her work. I cry hello.

She gives her dressing gown a shake,
And even though her finger aches.
She works so hard without a break,
From dawn til dusk while she's awake.

The dressing gown is fluffy, warm and deep,
But she has promises to keep,
Once taken off its for the cat to sleep.
Sweet dreams come to him thinking of a bird cheep.

She rises from her giant bed,
With thoughts of the day in her head,
She eats her jam with lots of bread.
Ready for the day ahead.

Everyday is a you day

Mondays are for bank holidays and picnics in
the boot
Tuesdays are for flower arranging with odd
numbers
Wednesdays are for farrier days and always
ending up last
Thursdays are for trips to Dewhursts for Chinese
stir fry
Fridays are for good ones swinging Grace at
Wallington
Saturdays are for coffee shops
Sundays are for ponies and poo picking and, of
course, garden centres

Because everyday is a you day

MOTHERHOOD

Many unpaid tasks

Opening jars, reading homework, filling flasks

Those not even hers are taken under her wing

Her offspring are everything

Each day is no longer her own

Recalling memories in person or on the phone

Help is always at hand

Offering advise her children understand

Overprotection is standard, all she needs is her stares

Days turn to weeks, which turn to month, that turn to years

My Mam

Thoughtful and helpful
Determined and loyal
Always makes me smile

She lives within me

11

She's the colour of the brightest daffodil
She smells like ponies
She tastes like a delicious a soft loaf of bread
She sounds like rain on a glass roof
She feels like a cheeky tickle
She looks like the shimmer on a swimming pool
She lives within me

That bus adventure

The bus where passengers journeyed together
Trundling down the passing road
Trembling against the weather
Those aboard minds in overload

Between Newcastle and Paris they went
Breathes held and lips sealed
Bizarre stories around who was present
Being guarded with the opinions they shield

Arrival came and went with memories made
Amazing shows and rides through the days
Among the travellers' expectations were slayed
A toilet, some medication and even the bus
decays

Everyone made it home
Each story was filled with fun
Embracing the disasters into this poem
Even the next adventure reminds this one can't
be outdone

It's our story of course

I hear stories and tales
I smell corned beef pie and microwave sponge
cake
I see pets and daffodils
I feel cuddles and many, many tickles
I taste dust from Bill and sandy sandwiches

What is it?
It's our story of course

I would thank you

I would thank you
day or night
I would thank you
when I get a fright
I would thank you
for your help
I would thank you
when I yelp
In the yard or while you squeeze a spot
'cause that was as important
as going for a trot

Thank you for always being you!

Didactic Cinquain of a mother

Mother
Dedicated, determined
Discover, engage, illuminate
Unreservedly the best
Giver

Roses are red

Roses are Red
Violets are Blue
My mother is better
Than any of you

The Sue Clerihew

17

A Mam called Sue
Made me me, as I grew
A lady that never would boast
Likes some delicious seeded toast

Cat-Alan

A had myself a mother
As perfect as could be
I thought she'd like to gain a pet
To keep her company
I sent him for one night
With a blanket for a bed
But now he sleeps right next to her
Quite often on her head

I will never be a Mam like you

I will never be a Mam like you
You give more than anyone I know

I will never be a Mam like you
You have endless creative ideas

I will never be a Mam like you
You see the world honestly

I will never be a Mam like you
You find a solution for everything

I will never be a Mam like you
You are truly irreplaceable

I will never be a Mam like you
You work and work and work some more

I will never be a Mam like you
You always know just what to do

99%

Ninety nine percent
Dedicated or crazy
A horsey Mam knows

Pets and so much more

21

Horses and courses
Rabbits and habits
Dogs and logs
Stick insects and projects
Cats and facts

I have you

Africa has a Moeder
Albania has a Nene
Belarus has a Matka
Bosnia has a Majko
Croatia has a Mati
Denmark has a Mor
Estonia has an Ema
Finland has an Aiti
France has a Mere
Germany has a Mutter
Greece has a Mana
Hawaii has a Makuahine
Italy has a Madre
Japan has an Okaasan
Lithuania has a Motina
Norway has a Mamma
Poland has a Matka
Turkey has an Anne
I have you, my Mam

Forever is loved

23

A mother with love
For her daughter and hers too
Forever is loved